~ DISGUSTING HISTORY ~

The Bloody, Rotten Roman Empire

THE DISGUSTING DETAILS | ANCIENT ROME

by James A. Corrick

Consultant:
Richard S. Williams
Associate Professor of History
Washington State University
Pullman, Washington

CAPSTONE PRESS
a capstone imprint

Fact Finders are published by Capstone Press,
151 Good Counsel Drive, P.O. Box 669, Mankato, Minnesota 56002.
www.capstonepub.com

032010
005740CGF10

Books published by Capstone Press are manufactured with paper
containing at least 10 percent post-consumer waste.

Library of Congress Cataloging-in-Publication Data
Corrick, James A.
  The bloody, rotten Roman Empire : the disgusting details about life in ancient Rome / by James A. Corrick.
     p. cm.—(Fact finders. Disgusting history.)
     Summary: "Describes disgusting details about daily life in ancient Rome, including housing, food, and
sanitation"—Provided by publisher.
     Includes bibliographical references and index.
     ISBN 978-1-4296-4541-6 (library binding)
     1. Rome—Civilization—Juvenile literature. I. Title. II. Series.

DG77.C67 2011
937—dc22   2010004413

Editorial Credits
Mari Bolte, editor; Alison Thiele and Gene Bentdahl, designers; Wanda Winch, media researcher;
   Eric Manske, production specialist

Photo Credits
Alamy: Lebrecht Music and Arts Photo Library, 7, North Wind Picture Archives, 26, World History
Archive, 25, 27; The Art Archive: NGS Image Collection/H.M. Herget, 14 (top); The Bridgeman Art Library
International: Index/Louvre, Paris, France, 21; Capstone: Chris Forsey, 5 (btm); Getty Images Inc: De
Agostini Picture Library/De Agostini, 16, The Bridgeman Art Library International/Fedor Andreevich
Bronnikov, 22, The Bridgeman Art Library International/Private Collection, 12; The Granger Collection,
New York, 19 (top); iStockphoto: Alan Tobey, 14 (btm); Johnny Shumate, cover; Mary Evans Picture Library,
8, 23; North Wind Picture Archives, 11, 29; Nova Development Corporation, 4 (top right), 5 (top); Shutterstock:
akva, 19 (btm), 26 (btm), Asier Villafrance, 4 (btm right), Dianna Toney, 4 (middle), freelanceartist, grunge
design, ppl, 4 (btm left), Turi Tamas, Fact box design element

Primary Source Bibliography
Page 19—as published in *De Medicina* by Aulus Cornelius Celsus (Cambridge, Mass.: Harvard
   University Press, 1935–38).
Page 26—from *The Deeds of the Divine Augustus* by Augustus, as published in *The Gladiators: History's Most
Deadly Sport* by Fik Meijer and translated by Liz Walters (New York: Thomas Dunne Books, 2005).

TABLE OF CONTENTS

ROME
753 BC–AD 476

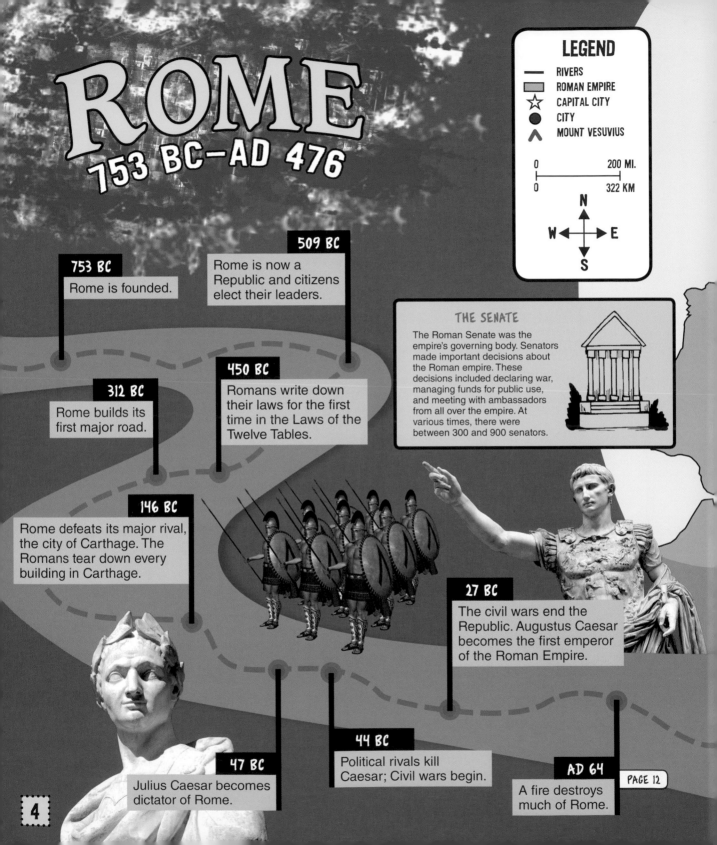

PAGE 12

LEGEND

— RIVERS
▭ ROMAN EMPIRE
☆ CAPITAL CITY
● CITY
⋀ MOUNT VESUVIUS

0 — 200 MI.
0 — 322 KM

N
W ← → E
S

753 BC
Rome is founded.

509 BC
Rome is now a Republic and citizens elect their leaders.

312 BC
Rome builds its first major road.

450 BC
Romans write down their laws for the first time in the Laws of the Twelve Tables.

THE SENATE

The Roman Senate was the empire's governing body. Senators made important decisions about the Roman empire. These decisions included declaring war, managing funds for public use, and meeting with ambassadors from all over the empire. At various times, there were between 300 and 900 senators.

146 BC
Rome defeats its major rival, the city of Carthage. The Romans tear down every building in Carthage.

27 BC
The civil wars end the Republic. Augustus Caesar becomes the first emperor of the Roman Empire.

47 BC
Julius Caesar becomes dictator of Rome.

44 BC
Political rivals kill Caesar; Civil wars begin.

AD 64
A fire destroys much of Rome.

BRITAIN

GAUL

RHINE RIVER

DANUBE RIVER

ATLANTIC
OCEAN

ITALY

SPAIN

CORSICA

TIBER R.

ADRIATIC SEA

CONSTANTINOPLE

SARDINIA

ROME

POMPEII

GREECE

SICILY

ATHENS

CARTHAGE

MEDITERRANEAN SEA

THE COLOSSEUM
Construction on the Colosseum was completed in AD 80. The arena stood 171 feet (52 meters) high. Seventy-six public entries led to 48 sections of seating. Spectators were given tickets showing their exact section, row, and seat number.

ROMAN EMPIRE BY THE NUMBERS, AD 250

300 MILLION—number of people in the world

65 MILLION—number of people living under the Roman Empire

1,000,000—number of people living in the city of Rome

500,000—number of slaves living in the city of Rome

600—number of senators

1—number of emperors who ruled Rome

AD 324
Constantinople founded as Eastern capital.

AD 80
PAGE 24
The Roman Colosseum opens.

AD 476
The fall of Rome. Last western emperor overthrown.

AD 79
The volcano Mount Vesuvius destroys the Roman city of Pompeii.

AD 391
Christianity becomes the religion of Rome.

FILTHY STREETS

Two thousand years ago, the Roman Empire ruled all the lands that bordered the Mediterranean Sea. The ancient Romans had many tools that helped make their lives easier. But there were also parts of Roman life that were dirty, gross, or even deadly.

The Romans grew rich off their empire. Gold, silver, and other treasures flowed into the city. There were large public buildings and many expensive homes. There was also a sports arena and two racetracks.

But Rome was not all gold and riches. Garbage filled the streets in the poorer parts of the city. There was also plenty of human and animal waste. Only the very rich had running water. Human waste piled up outside apartment buildings. Animals lived on the streets, dropping waste as they moved about.

Shops lined the streets of ancient Rome.

FOUL FACT

People killed their animals on the street. The animal remains were tossed in the sewer.

FOUL FACT

Rome was a messy place. Citizens produced more than 110,000 pounds (50,000 kilograms) of solid waste every day.

Rome's sewers emptied into the nearby Tiber River. Rainwater was supposed to wash the waste from the sewers into the river. There were big openings on the street for people to dump waste into the sewers. The holes did nothing to hide the stench coming from them.

Few homes had toilets. Some people paid to use public toilets, which were set up over the sewers. Other people used chamber pots.

By law Romans were supposed to empty the chamber pots into a sewer drain. But some people lived in tall apartment buildings. They did not want to carry smelly pots down the many stairs to the drains. So they just emptied the pots out their windows. People passing by were sometimes showered in waste.

There were laws against throwing bodily fluids out the window. Because there were no streetlights, the laws were impossible to enforce at night.

The garbage and animal waste mixed together on the streets. Everyone walked in this slimy mess. Workers were hired by the city to keep the streets clean. But the sewage would always build up again.

The Tiber River was polluted with garbage and human waste.

CITIZENS AND SLAVES

In Rome there were free people and slaves. Many of the free people were Roman citizens. Other free people included foreigners, merchants, or diplomats.

Although Roman women were citizens, they had fewer rights than men. Women could own property. But they could not vote or hold government offices. Women had male **guardians** all their lives. The guardians were usually husbands or male relatives.

The wealthiest Roman citizens had power over the poor. Rich Romans bought and sold goods throughout the empire. They even bought and sold people.

Thousands of slaves worked in and around Rome. Slaves were bought and sold at auctions. There they were stripped naked and kept in pens. This way, potential buyers could see for themselves that the slaves were healthy.

Some slaves were treated well. A few were paid, and some gained their freedom. But for most, life as a slave was horrible. Some slaves killed their babies at birth rather than allow them to become slaves.

guardian: someone who carefully watches and protects another person

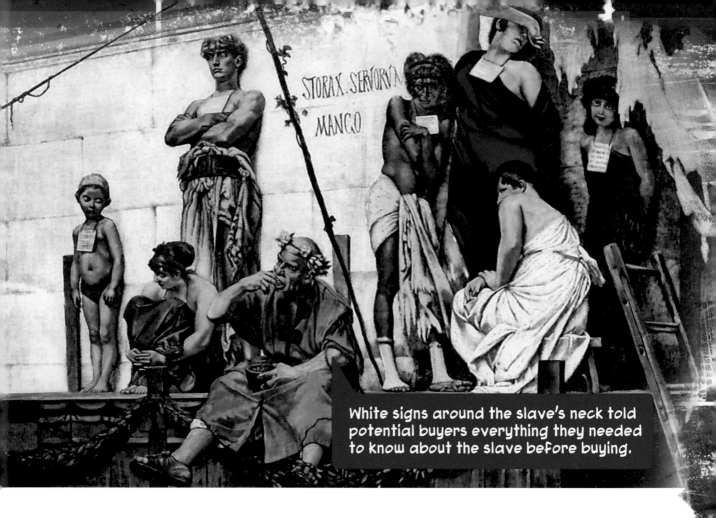

White signs around the slave's neck told potential buyers everything they needed to know about the slave before buying.

Some owners branded or tattooed their slaves' faces. Other slaves were bound with heavy neck chains or collars so they could not escape. Some slaves had to wear tags that showed their masters' names.

There was nothing fair in the treatment of slaves. An owner could beat, torture, or kill a slave for any reason. One Roman broke the legs of a slave who annoyed him. A slave who killed his owner was put to death. But so were all the other slaves in the household—men, women, and children.

FOUL FACT

In AD 64, a fire swept through Rome. The city's wooden buildings fed the flames that burned for six days and seven nights.

Many ancient Romans ate their meals at food stands beneath their apartment buildings.

DEADLY HOMES

After a long day at work, imagine coming home to find three people sleeping in your bed! It might seem crowded, but ancient Romans were used to it.

At one time, the city of Rome was home to more than 1 million people. Most Romans lived in apartment buildings above shops. The poorest people shared rooms on the highest stories. Some buildings were eight or nine stories high. These buildings were not safe. The first floor or two might be made of sturdy stone. But the higher stories were often made only of mud and wood. Many buildings fell under their own weight. Those unlucky enough to be in a collapsing building often died.

Apartment buildings also burned down. Although cooking inside the apartments was discouraged, some people did it anyway. Carelessly tended flames from lamps or cooking fires could have a horrible effect. The buildings were built with mud brick and timber that caught on fire easily and burned quickly. There were no fire alarms or fire escapes. People on the highest floors often died.

Building owners rarely cared about these deaths. One owner was actually happy that one of his buildings collapsed. He planned to rebuild and charge higher rents.

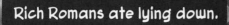

Rich Romans ate lying down.

FOUL FACT

Guests at a Roman dinner party might snack on grasshoppers, grubs, or animal parts.

NASTY MEALS

Imagine showing up to a friend's house for dinner. Instead of burgers and fries, you're served snails and pig's stomach! Romans couldn't just go to a restaurant or grocery store to get their meals. Food came from farms all over the empire.

Most Romans ate simple meals. The poorest ate bread or porridge with vegetables. Those with more money sometimes had fish. Few Romans ate meat, which was too expensive.

The wealthy, of course, ate well. They threw fancy dinner parties that lasted for hours. Some Romans went broke trying to impress their friends.

The hosts served strange food. Unusual dishes at these parties included ostrich or peacock. Tongue and brains were eaten along with the meat. Sometimes mice were used as stuffing for birds or other animals. A favorite dish was a small bird called the figpecker. Diners ate all parts of this bird except its beak.

Both rich and poor Romans used olive oil for cooking and flavoring. But even more popular was garum. This sauce was made from aged fish heads, fins, and guts. It was poured over most foods and even used as a medicine.

GRASSHOPPERS

KEEPING CLEAN

Bath time! It's time to climb into the tub—with 1,500 other people. Being clean was important to Romans. Many people bathed daily at public bathhouses. They sat in warm pools or steam rooms. While soaking, people visited and did business. Men and women bathed at different times.

There were hot baths and cold baths. Slaves heated the baths beneath the floor with wood fires. **Aqueducts** brought in 198,130 gallons (750,000 liters) of fresh spring water a day.

Romans did not have soap. Instead, they rubbed themselves with olive oil. Then they scraped themselves clean with a curved metal tool. The oil helped remove dirt.

aqueduct: a bridge built to carry water

Everyone was encouraged to bathe at the bath houses, including the poor and the sick.

Without soap, Romans had to find other ways to clean their clothes. They made up a cleaner that used human urine. It worked. To collect the pee, laundry workers set out pots on the street. Roman men would relieve themselves into these pots. The dirty clothes were soaked and scrubbed in vats of urine.

The baths and laundries did not keep the Romans safe from fleas and lice. Dirty streets and homes helped keep the number of pests high. Romans had no way to rid themselves of these annoying creatures. People tried getting rid of the pesky bugs by rubbing themselves with dog fat or drinking a concoction that included bits of dead skin.

FOUL FACT

The emperors Nero and Vespasian put a tax on urine. The urine was collected from pots and then sold, usually to laundries or leather shops.

DISEASE AND DOCTORS

Romans were in constant danger from sickness and infection. Roman doctors, who did not understand what caused disease, could do little to stop outbreaks. Many people caught **malaria**. Sometimes people got **smallpox**. Thousands became sick and died every year. Only 50 percent of children survived to become adults.

Got a headache? Drink some goat dung soup. That was just one of the many odd medicines Romans used. Roman doctors had a wide variety of medicines, mainly herbs. But there were many treatments that did not work. Romans routinely took pills made from dried bugs or crushed-up snakes. Swellings were packed with animal waste.

Many doctors were self-taught. In fact, any man with some tools and herbs could claim he was a doctor. While there were a number of good doctors, there were also many frauds. Poor Romans did not have the luxury to be picky about who treated them.

malaria: a serious disease that people get from mosquito bites

smallpox: a contagious disease that causes chills, fever, and pimples that scar

Pain and the Doctor

Now a surgeon should be youthful ... with a strong and steady hand which never trembles ... with vision sharp and clear, and spirit undaunted; filled with pity, so that he wishes to cure his patient, yet is not moved by his cries, to go too fast, or cut less than is necessary; but he does everything just as if the cries of pain cause him no emotion.

Aulus Cornelius Celsus
Doctor and author of De Medicina

19

Certain animals were sacrificed to each god. Bulls, rams, and boars were acceptable gifts for gods.

sacrifice: an offering made to a god

altar: a large table used for religious ceremonies

BLOODY SACRIFICES

The Romans worshipped many gods and goddesses. Popular gods were Jupiter and his wife, Juno. Mars and Venus also had many followers. Rulers often claimed gods or goddesses as their ancestors.

Romans made **sacrifices** to important gods. It was hoped that the gods would be pleased with the gifts. The most common sacrifice was a goat or a cow. A priest would kill the animal and would search the liver for messages from the gods. Then he burned the liver, fat, guts, and bones on the god's **altar**. After the ceremony, the Romans cooked and ate the rest of the animal.

Roman families had their own household gods. These gods protected the family from harm. They were given gifts of grain or wine and received part of a family's meal.

Romans held many official religious events throughout the year. In the middle of February, priests sacrificed several goats and a dog to the god Pan. This celebration was held to represent the founding of Rome. In October Romans would hold the October Horse, a chariot race held in honor of the god Mars. A priest killed one of the winning horses and cut off its head. Two teams fought over the head, which was thought to bring good luck.

CRIME AND PUNISHMENT

Romans who broke the law could end up losing their lives. There were many kinds of punishments, but jail time was not one of them. The Romans used prisons only to hold prisoners before their trial or punishment.

Citizens could not be given physical punishment for minor crimes like forgery or lying. Instead, guilty citizens might have to pay a fine or leave Rome. Sometimes they were sent to live alone on small islands. Those who committed major crimes, like treason or murder, might have their heads cut off. Others could be thrown from a cliff known as the Tarpeian Rock.

Noncitizens faced harsher punishments, like being whipped. The Roman whip had three strands of leather. Each strand was braided with lead balls or sharp pieces of metal. It was sometimes used to beat a criminal to death.

Hanging from a cross was considered the most disgraceful way to die.

Death was the penalty for crimes like treason, murder, stealing, and arson. Arsonists were burned alive. But one of the worst forms of death was being tied or nailed to a wooden cross. The victim often died slowly and painfully. Only foreigners and slaves could be whipped to death, burned alive, or hung on a cross.

People who committed crimes against Rome were thrown off Tarpeian Rock.

DEADLY SPORTS

Romans enjoyed deadly sports. Competitors took the field knowing they might not leave alive. Emperors and other rich citizens paid to organize the games. Arenas like the Colosseum attracted audiences from all around Rome. More than 50,000 people packed the Colosseum to watch these deadly contests.

Most gladiators were either slaves or prisoners of war. But a few were citizens who fought for respect. Just like today's pro athletes, successful gladiators received star treatment. Women saw them as extremely attractive. Declarations of love were scribbled on walls of the gladiator schools.

Gladiators experienced tough training at special schools. Fighters pledged to endure humiliation and death without protest. But for some, gladiator school seemed like a good choice. They were fed three meals a day, received medical care, and had the chance for fame and money. If they survived long enough, they could even win their freedom.

FOUL FACT

The bodies of people and smaller animals killed at the Colosseum were often dumped into the Tiber River.

Gladiators were expected to die with honor.

At the arena, wild animals battled each other or armed men in the morning. Planners of the games traveled far and wide to find wild animals for the Colosseum. Creatures like rhinos and bears were brought in from great distances. Many animals were killed this way.

In the afternoon, men condemned to death were brought in to fight. Sometimes they were pitted against each other. Other times they battled trained gladiators. The criminals rarely won. The winner's prize was to keep fighting until someone killed him.

Animals in the Arena

Three times I held gladiator games in my own name and five times in the name of my sons or grandsons. During the games, around 10,000 men fought each other to the death … Twenty-six times I presented the people with hunting shows with wild animals from Africa … and in them around 3,500 animals were killed.

Emperor Augustus (27 BC–AD 14)
From The Deeds of the Divine Augustus

Deaths were common at the Circus Maxiumus.

Romans took their bloody games to the racetrack too. There were several racetracks throughout Rome. The Circus Maximus was the most popular track. It could seat 100,000 fans. Chariots pulled by four horses were crowd favorites.

Horses tore around the track at full speed. They ran all-out for seven laps, or 5 miles (8 kilometers). There were sharp turns at the corners and frequent crashes. Drivers were sometimes dragged to their deaths. They could also be crushed under hooves or wheels.

BATTLE WOUNDS

Soldiers in the Roman army had a rough life. It was the army's job to protect Rome from attack. There was no room for failure, and punishments were harsh. New army recruits and the weakest soldiers were placed at the frontline during battles. This position helped them gain more experience. It also prevented them from running away in fear.

Battle wounds were nasty. The soldiers fought with swords and spears. They also carried large shields. Both Roman and enemy weapons sliced deep into arms and legs. A strong blow from a sword could split a soldier's head open. Spear thrusts could cause fatal wounds.

Roman military training was tough. Beating with thick sticks was a common punishment. Sometimes a commanding officer ordered a soldier beaten to death. Occasionally the soldier's head was cut off afterward. Deserters were usually nailed to a cross. When large groups of soldiers deserted, the punishment was harsh. The commanding officer selected every 10th man. The other soldiers then beat the selected men until they died.

Whether you were a soldier, gladiator, slave, or citizen, life was dirty, disgusting, and deadly in ancient Rome!

Roman soldiers fought their enemies at close range.

GLOSSARY

altar (AWL-tur)—a large table used for religious ceremonies

aqueduct (AK-wuh-duhkt)—a large bridge built to carry water from a mountain into the valley

arson (AR-suhn)—the act of setting a fire on purpose in order to damage property or people

contaminate (kuhn-TA-muh-nayt)—to make dirty or unfit for use

diplomat (DI-pluh-mat)—a person sent by a government to represent it in another country

forgery (FORJ-ree)—the crime of making illegal copies of paintings, money, or other valuable objects

guardian (GAR-dee-uhn)—someone who carefully watches and protects something

malaria (muh-LAIR-ee-uh)—a serious disease that people get from mosquito bites; malaria causes high fever, chills, and sometimes death

sacrifice (SAK-ruh-fisse)—a gift of something valuable given to honor a god

smallpox (SMAWL-poks)—a disease that spreads easily from person to person, causing chills, fever, and pimples that scar

treason (TREE-zuhn)—the act of betraying one's country

READ MORE

DiPrimio, Pete. *How'd They Do That in Ancient Rome?* How'd They Do That. Hockessin, Del.: Mitchell Lane, 2010.

Hanel, Rachael. *Ancient Rome: An Interactive History Adventure*. You Choose: Historical Eras. Mankato, Minn: Capstone Press, 2010.

Malam, John. *Ancient Rome*. Time Travel Guides: Raintree Freestyle Express. Chicago: Raintree, 2008.

Scurman, Ike, and John Malam. *Ancient Roman Civilization*. Ancient Civilizations and Their Myths and Legends. New York: Rosen, 2010.

INTERNET SITES

FactHound offers a safe, fun way to find Internet sites related to this book. All of the sites on FactHound have been researched by our staff.

Here's all you do:

Visit www.facthound.com

Type in this code: 9781429645416

INDEX